THE LESSON OF PLUMS

THE LESSON OF PLUMS

Lois Parker Edstrom

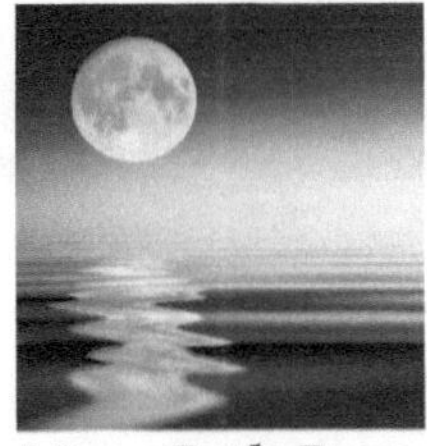

MoonPath Press

Poetry
ISBN 978-1-936657-55-1

Cover photo "Summer Plums" © by Ronda Broatch
For more from this artist, go to:
https://fineartamerica.com/profiles/ronda-broatch.html

Author photo by Mel Edstrom

Book design by Tonya Namura using Genium Basic

MoonPath Press is dedicated to publishing the finest poets living in the U.S. Pacific Northwest.

MoonPath Press
PO Box 445
Tillamook, OR 97141

MoonPathPress@gmail.com

http://MoonPathPress.com

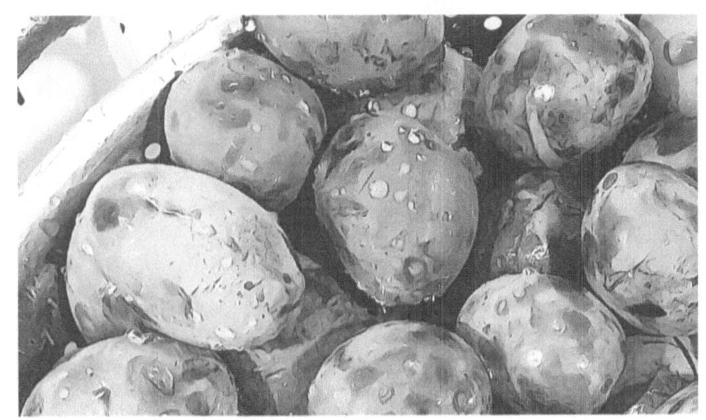

FOR MEL
love and gratitude beyond measure

TABLE OF CONTENTS

THE LESSON OF PLUMS

ONE

Look at how a single candle can both defy and define the darkness.

~ Anne Frank

FRAGILE WINGS

As long as you have mystery you have health.
~ G.K. Chesterton

They say paradox is the tension between things
that don't make sense.

The big questions of a triune God, the rhythm
of seasons, the distance between the beginning
and the end.

Surrounded by mystery, my mind explores
on fragile wings.

The miracle of bodies—a delicate balance
of hormones and chemistry, impossibly born,
departure to the unknown on a final breath.

The disposition of love—what sets it on its journey,
keeps it trudging through years of joy
and hardship and pain?

What of the muse, the generous midwife, that coaxes
concertos, novels, paintings, to life?

How a baby toddles through the maze of language
and finds a voice.

How the spider, a famed architect, builds
its stunning geometric structure, sets lines
so delicate, yet strong.

How finches know to wait on the garden fence
on the day snap peas push through the soil.

Why a single pink poppy grows in the ditch
along Mossy Rock Road.

I say, live the tension. Let the stories be strange.

DEEP

Listen to the silence. Can you hear
the earth humming its mysterious tune?
Can you feel the vibration of stars,
the pulse of tides?

Scientists probe the silent darkness
of ocean depths. Watery images
float to the surface: schools of glistening
fish, a palette of breathtaking colors.
Strange creatures, disguised
to disappear into their surroundings,
some predatory, others hidden
for self-protection.

Imagine creatures so long in darkness,
no need for eyes. Some blind,
some navigating by their own
bioluminescent light.

Frilled sharks, translucent ghost fish,
twelve-foot spider crab, black dragon
fish, sparkling jewel squid, and delicate
strands of harp sponges.

Profound silence, even when veiled
in darkness, may lead to unexpected
places, an inward journey that invites
us to listen. To go deep is to realize
how much we don't understand, yet
such unimaginable beauty.

THE QUIET CORE OF CHAOS

We live amid chaos whether we recognize
it or not. I choose to live on an island
away from the blare and glare of the city

yet our island emerged from a violent birth,
rising from the depths of the sea, its craggy
face presenting a few miles distant from its

mainland mother. Volcanic eruptions
scattered agates along the shore,
a sudden disruptive upheaval.

The revelations of wind, the epiphany
of stars burning from the inside, blinking
their ancient stories into the shifting air.

Truth is always a bit odd. How meaning
may be found in the midst of chaos if
we listen, open ourselves to the risk

of what we might find inside. And isn't this
what art is all about?

THE LESSON OF PLUMS

After year-long illness, a dream.
My doctor stands in the center
of a cultivated field,
the furrows deep and straight.
His brown suit blends
with the richness of the dark soil.
Arms extended, palms open,
his words travel through
sunlit air: You are ready to grow.

So simple, so hackneyed,
yet when I awake I know it's over,
the illness that blew in
like a menacing wind and me
a trembling leaf clinging
to what I knew of strength—
now nearly floating
in an autonomy of lightness.

Sometimes it's not about
seeking but of receiving,
the way a plum takes in light,
an inner ripening that cracks
its perfect purple skin,
and sweetness, an amber rivulet,
crusts along the gash.

RED GIANTS AND WHITE DWARFS

For my part I know nothing with any certainty,
but the sight of the stars makes me dream.
~ Vincent van Gogh

For Emily

How can we know except by listening?
There is no certainty, no certainty at all,
except what hums to us through the mists
of our dreams, speaks through the voice of silence.

My granddaughter and I exchange quotes,
this quiet girl who travels beyond
her years, bonded by a longing
we cannot name.

We look to the stars, those burning
embers that fuel our yearnings,
that glitter in our imaginations:
red giants and white dwarfs.

Yes, how can we know except by listening?
They say stars are in constant conflict
with themselves: the gravity of collapsing inward,
the light that pushes back.

EMERGING FROM DARKNESS

Blood Moon, January 20, 2019

Tonight, we are the darkness between sun and moon,
insignificant in the reflected glow, yet we cast
a large shadow.

The earth's eyes turn skyward, and I wonder
what the ancients thought when they saw
a blood moon in an inky sky.

A perfect citrus sphere, blood orange, rimmed
in golden light, the color appearing only after
the full eclipse has told its story.

So like our journeys through difficult times
when we must move through darkness
to find light.

As if on cue, stars appear through dark velvet curtains,
take bows on the night's stage, and we,
an awestruck audience, offer an ovation of silence.

AND THEY DANCED BY THE LIGHT OF THE MOON

Sly old moon, familiarity has not breached
your mysteries. You hold onto your secrets.
I am continually beguiled by the gleam
and shadow of your orbits.

A charismatic luminary, you pull us
toward you and we are helpless to resist.
Inner tides ebb and flow; the sea's
moods are faithful to your call.

You rise, cloaked in melancholy,
and I love that feeling, just on the edge
of sadness where I have no voice,
yet syllables arrange themselves
turning, tumbling into space
and I whisper, *Tell me, tell me.*

EBEY'S LANDING

Whidbey Island

I come to the shore when demands of everyday
grow heavy, float on waves of stillness,
calmed by rhythms of the sea.

The *time between* this and then—
a quiet moment when day fades into night,
or a clutch of seasons that span a lifetime.

I wait, standing on the edge
of the unknown—time salted with intensity,
serenity, hopefulness, uncertainty.

How to wait, yet capture the moment? How to
savor change, yet cling to the authenticity
of the fixed?

Is it longing for something beyond myself
that ripples deep within the mysterious
well of possibilities?

The poet says, *Don't try too hard. Just be.*
Slow down the words. See how light
informs the sea, how it plays counterpoint

to the tide, and mountains ghost to the horizon.

IMPLICATIONS OF GLASS

Answers to big questions rarely arrive
in one piece. Hints, even signs or signals,
rub against our intellect and we may,
or may not, catch the shine of their truth.

The bowl of sea glass on my library table
glistens in sunlight; broken shards tumbled
over stones for decades, now shaped
and transformed, speak of the past: a brown
spirits bottle, a cobalt blue liniment jar,
a green soda bottle, and turquoise bottles
that once held old-time elixirs.

Like tumbled glass, fragments of answers
may hide in everyday slices of life;
we just need time to put the pieces together.
Or, insight may be colored by lessons
from the past when we were buffeted
by tides of hardship and loss.

Yet, at times, a flash of knowing
comes suddenly. I think of this
as I hold a kaleidoscope to light
one turn and tiny bits of glass fall
into place, fitting together perfectly.

OMINOUS BEAUTY

I've never known how to deal
with the reverberations of beauty.
Its impact is almost cruel:
the inadequacy of words,
the isolation of silence.

Traveling into the mountains,
over the North Cascade Pass,
I see hushed forests, deep gorges,
jade-colored lakes, Rowan berries
that shout against a background
of evergreens, the ominous beauty
of ancient, jagged peaks.

What is it about beauty that creates
such longing? It requires nothing,
yet evokes a response.
Those who went before had the pleasure
of naming: *Early Winters, Golden Horn,*
Liberty Bell Mountain, Snagtooth Ridge,
Goat Creek, Lost River, Rainy Day Pass,

and by naming, a way to hold on,
bring the unattainable closer, become
a part of something the other side
of our understanding. Yet this glory,
this wild beauty, can never be conveyed,
and I am breathless with trying.

APPLES OF WINTER

They hang on the trees
in the deep of winter. Once crisp
and red as Sleeping Beauty's lips,
they are a fairy tale drama.

They do not fall, they are not picked.
Neglected, they are left to rot,
until what is brown and soft
seeps away. This could be the end
of the story.

But, the prince of the north had arrived
earlier and, unnoticed, touched the apples
with the passion of winter, encasing
their smooth surfaces in ice.

What we know of certainty slipped away
with the juices of decay. Now exact
icy replicas dangle from the trees—
ghost apples—ethereal vessels of light.
Too perfect for this world.

WINTER ART

For Kurt

Winter slices everything down to bare basics.
Clouds darken and sunlight, weak and pale
as the face of fear, slips out between shifting shadows.

Sodden leaves clump along roadsides
and bunch in porch corners. But oh, the sculptural
beauty of bare willow and alder and birch.

Thin branches touch and overlap forming
intricate triangles of light.
What is it that you find beautiful? a friend asks

as I raise my face to the tops of the denuded,
exposed trees that flare against the sky.
I consider how something made vulnerable

exposes its beauty, and the empty spaces—
a latticework of branches—how one must look
through and beyond the obvious to find what is true.

LANDSCAPE OF SILENCE

The island speaks without words. Visitors,
as they look out over Admiralty Inlet, sunlight
shimmering on the water, say, *It's peaceful—*

a blue-green bowl of reflection
and light to illuminate what's within.
I'm learning to listen, breathe the stillness;

breath by breath I'm filled, yet somehow
launched on a search for more,
an exploration of an inner landscape

where surprises rise and challenge
shadowy truths, sincere beliefs;
where silence, a guide to authenticity,

a mentor, comforts and inspires. At night
the island's silence makes me wary,
teaches the need for caution

and the harshness of hunger, its tranquility
shattered by the yips and howls of ravenous
coyotes, by the owl's soundless, deadly flight.

HIDDEN PERILS

This morning Mt. Rainier appears
out of the mist, a solid unchanging
presence, yet we know of the danger
within: turbulent movement, molten rock,
sporadic steam that escapes in hovering clouds.

We live in the midst of unseen dangers,
some remote, some within. How to balance
risk on the scales of serenity?

Each morning deer graze in our fields,
stop by for apples, bringing their newborn fawns:
the delicate hoofs, trusting eyes, long lashes.

Somehow, although tranquility illuminates them,
they are always alert: ears pricked at a sound
beyond that of a human's recognition

and the absolute stillness as their eyes focus
on a distant concern. They reside within
the threat of the coyotes' ruthless hunger,

yet when they fold themselves down to rest
it is as if they give themselves completely to peace.

ART NOUVEAU

Dragonfly, Wood Block Print
~ Francy Blumhagen

Night and the dragonfly
in the block print near the bed
flies into dreamy abstraction,
its webbed wings blue-black
iridescence, like a veil
of moonlight through darkness.

Stitched into European folktales
as the devil's darning needle,
troll's spindle,
adder's servant,
a shadowy flashing stylet
despised and feared.

It alights on a temple bell
in a Kobe garden;
the wings, like mantilla lace,
brush the bright face
of a sunflower in Oaxaca.
Here a mark of renewal,
courage, and strength,
this double-barred cross
rests with wings open.
Can we risk such vulnerability?

CONFESSION

I am a syntaxer.
My sins are many.
I tax mostly myself.

I arrange symbols, hungering
for harmony; chase a relentless
notion that my marrow-language
matters.

Words pulse toward each other,
float into shuttered dreams
tangled amid half-thoughts
and desires I sort through
searching for connections.

I struggle to honor inexpressible
feelings as I touch
a pussy willow bud, listen
to the hum of bees, notice
a sick man without stockings
hunched against a building.

Day and night words skitter
over keys, tumbling locks
that link past with present.
I gather some in a vault
of safekeeping, hoard others
in recessed chambers,
exposing them one by one
knowing they will
also expose me.

Taxed by words,
urged by words,

assuaged by words,
lexis bound: a syntaxer
showing no sign of remorse.

THE WEIGHT OF WORDS

I'm trying to become more thoughtful
about spoken words; words that fly
into the air like broken-winged birds,

unlikely to soar on uplifted currents
of wisdom, perhaps to glide toward
a landscape of kindness and light.

Often, I choose silence,
an inner dialogue that considers
what I know of truth,

and I listen to what's said and not
said: sentences bent around the truth,
snapped in half and left hanging,

silence that can initiate a storm.
Bonhoeffer said, *Not to speak
is to speak*—those times

when words must carry the burden
of justice. So, what to set aside
and what to carry to the altar

of integrity? A daunting decision
knowing one may send blessings
or blight into the world.

I'm learning to be more cautious
before I speak, recalling that even eagles
exercise their wings before they fledge.

KINDNESS KNOWS NO SEASON

A real desire to believe all the good you can of others . . .
~ C.S. Lewis

Sometimes the divide is as wide and powerful as the
Columbia River
as it snakes its way through canyons and arid desert.

Narrow passages compress petty annoyances into roiling
disturbances: the guy who cuts you off in congested traffic,

someone walking too slowly when you are on the way
to an appointment, loud chewing at the table,

the casual diners who talk on the phone in a restaurant,
a discourteous clerk.

Aggravations clutter our lives with uncharitable
thoughts and *wish I could* plans of action.

We are like ants scurrying about, lifting more
than our share of grief. Can we allow

for some inconvenience? Discomfort?
This November afternoon the cove is still.

Only a soft breeze ripples its surface.
So much to learn from nature.

EVENTIDE

In the garden at twilight, the fragrance
of lavender mingles with the night air, clouds
deepening to purple.

My husband, clipping lilacs, straightens
from his task, alert, as if he hears a distant sound.
Profound hearing loss has isolated him

within seasons of silence. He has always loved
spring: the lengthening days, the first crocuses
and, most of all, bird song.

Now I sense he is aware of something beyond
the usual wall of silence. *I hear the birds,* he says.
New hearing devices, advanced technology,

have sprung him into spring and for the first time
in over ten years he listens to birds
settling into the night: avian vespers.

THE MANY WAYS OF LEAVING

His birth, like all births, a journey of separation
and reunion, then boyhood tides of distance

with the rightness of waves pulsing on the shore,
to leave, return, but never the same.

The premiere of his concerto, that night
in a dim concert hall, I watched him go.

Center stage, surrounded by orchestra,
tilted back from the concert grand, eyes closed,

music fired the impulses of his fingers,
muscles and tendons submissive to each note.

In that moment I knew: he went
to an unaccompanied place.

His concerto hung in the air, a satin canopy
of tasseled grace that swayed, dipped, lifted:

wild and pure as the agony of birth.

CONCERTO

For Brent

It courses through my body
like a river seeking the freedom
of the sea, a rhythm of inner tides
moving me to unexplored,
unexpected places.

Notes leap and tumble and soar,
waves that roll ashore from tranquil
waters or the roar of a gathering storm.

The melody rises, ripples out, and where
does it stop? It fills me, claims a part
of who I am, yet I cannot contain it.

Long after, unbidden in silence,
strains return, a memory wells up,
pulses as if summoned by the beat
of my heart, a quiet glorious reunion.

AN INTRICATE JOURNEY

My husband and I have been married
a long time, as have most of our friends.

It's not a boast—just the way it is.
Somehow, the two of us have made our way

through corridors of life together.
Missteps, wrong turns, celebratory arrivals.

Chambers filled with the light of memories
and stories and plans.

So curious, how a journey sustains itself,
when we rely on what we know to be true,

without access to the inner passages
of another's life.

Marriage is a ballroom of forgiveness.
How could it be otherwise?

Yet we dance under a brilliant chandelier
that sparkles and glows, loving so imperfectly.

WHEN A MIRACLE SPEAKS

When a miracle speaks, don't be bashful.
Run right up to it. Hug it like an old friend.
Don't let go. Give it an extra squeeze.

Walk the beach with it. Talk about old times,
those moments when the vessel of love
overflowed. Listen to every word.

When a miracle speaks, there are no thunderous
lightning bolts. Hold the drama. It speaks
from the back row. Look around. It may be
closer than you think.

Sometimes a miracle whispers. Other times
the miracle eats ice cream at midnight,
wears argyle socks and a fedora,
dances until the sun is up.

Don't forget the hard times. The miracle was there;
it was just wearing old jeans and sunglasses
so as not to be blinded by your tears.

Why are you so shy of miracles? You're not the only
mystery. You have a common rhythm. It's in your DNA.
Sometimes I think you enjoy being dull.

It's as simple as this: When a miracle
speaks, answer.

DAMP MAGIC

Consider the magical qualities of water.
Not the braided waterfalls that unfurl
down the mountain, the roar of the ocean,
nor the silvery slide of raindrops
cascading down the bedroom window.

Not even snowflakes, tiny frozen doilies
decorating the landscape, a white fairy tale
in a quiet world, or the gurgle
of a brook passing through a meadow.

Something curious happens in the shower,
while I'm rushing to get ready for a meeting;
bits and pieces of poems come gushing out,
infused in the hot water, and I fret
they will slip away, swirl down the drain,
before I can capture them.

Or while luxuriating in the bathtub,
words and images hook together,
float like clouds into the stream
of my consciousness, gauzy
irresistible lines of verse.

I'm sure I am not the only one
to experience the transforming power
of water, and what am I to do,
when the creative urge wraps me
in its big soft terry-cloth towel
and leads me, dripping, to my desk?

GEOMETRY OF FAITH

In dreams I see rich tapestries shot
with golden thread: rose, green, and silver

arabesque patterns, galvanic charm
that glides out of sleep into the sunrise

of consciousness and rises like a dove,
not of this world—bliss, unexplained

except for the subconscious truth of beauty
and who am I to question?

Later, on public television, I chance
upon familiar kaleidoscopic images,

breath-taking magnificence: Mandelbrot's Set—
budding, branching, complex geometry

that masters chaos—sunflowers, leaves,
shells, zebras, snowflakes, cauliflower,

geckos, brains, arranged in like patterns,
self-similarity, internal consistency.

Some call it the thumbprint of God,
a design that links all and goes on forever.

TWO

We are fragile creatures, and it is from this weakness, not despite it, that we discover the possibility of true joy.

~ Desmond Tutu

FAR AWAY DAUGHTERS

The rock sits on my desk, an odd rock—white
shot through with black veins, shaped like a potato.

I remember the day Cathy picked it up on the beach
at Ebey's Landing. Three of us, Cathy, her sister Kelli,

and I walked in bright sunlight that cast silver scales
on the incoming tide. We breathed deeply the briny air

blowing in off the Strait of Juan de Fuca as if we could
absorb the day and hold it close.

They call themselves my prodigal daughters,
although there is nothing imprudent about them.

It's a name I'm pleased to accept. Their mother,
my close friend, died when they were teenagers.

Many miles usually separate us, yet we are bound
together by more than the bond of loss

and we look like we belong together.
We all have red hair.

Cathy tells me, *Being together is to hear echoes*
of a time before griefs of all kinds set in.

Now, weeks later, I study the rock. I know she collects
objects from nature as touchstones of good memories.

The oversized rock is an unusual choice. Does it speak
to the largeness of the day or the heaviness of loss?

Its whiteness the brilliance of our time together
or its dark veins the remembrance of grief?

Perhaps some experiences are so immense they need
to be set aside for a while. In a note Cathy says,

I'll come get it—guaranteed. If you look closely
you can see mica chips

sparkling over the surface of the rock,
glittering like stars.

THE WORLD BETWEEN

Loss needs no introduction.
Uninvited, it visits everyone.
Like a ruthless river
that overflows its banks
it saturates all within its path,
changes course, creates
new channels, a new landscape
where nothing looks familiar.

Loss partners with change
the way wind alters the prospect
of clouds, transforming them
into new shapes, aligning
them with each other
in ever-changing compositions.

Loss questions what we knew
to be true, calls us to an unknown
perspective. How to find our way
suspended in a curious haze
of before and after? Perhaps we
must enter darkness to find light.

SYLLABLES OF WONDER

When I was a student nurse,
working in the newborn nursery,
our family doctor, from my small hometown,
came to the city hospital to check on a baby
who needed his attention.

Too bad about your grandmother, he said.
What about my grandmother?
Oh, I thought you knew. She had a stroke.

My dear grandmother who taught me
the language of the countryside. We picked
blackberries, gathered mushrooms, cut
and dried cascara bark.

I kneeled amid bleeding hearts and trillium
that grew rampant in the forest, a small child
learning to pray.

She taught the syllables of wonder
while Northern Lights spread watercolor
glory across the sky

and the delights of everyday
when we stood in the cold clear creek
as it washed summer dust from our feet.

Is it kind to withhold what might be hurtful?
Although my family thought to spare me,
they soon realized nothing could keep me
from her side.

KINTSUGI

Brokenness is not always obvious.
We don't hear the crack or splatter.

We wear an amulet of denial to protect
ourselves from the perceptions of others.

Is it possible we have been vulnerable
from the beginning, living within fragile shells?

A sudden blow, a series of subtle traumas,
may shatter our protection.

Unlike an egg dropped on a tile floor,
we have to believe we can be restored.

Perhaps we are not what we once were,
but we are not damaged.

Think of the Japanese who repair a broken vase
with gold, highlighting its flaws to add beauty

and, in so doing, the repaired vessel becomes
stronger.

A GLORIOUS WEBBING

It should be about the fragrance, but it's not.
It's about the sweet pea lashing itself
to the wire fence so tightly
tendrils must be cut to free the flower
and I'm drawn to the notion and need of bonds—

how a mother's arms and breast and voice
enclose the babe in a tender cocoon
of connection; how we link lives as we begin
an uncertain passage through crossroads of choice.

Friends have touched me with healing hands,
provided a cup of grace, pointed the way,
and waved me through. Do we really appreciate
how much we need each other?

C.S. Lewis said, *We read to know*
we are not alone. We need the comfort
of words to connect us to stories, intensely
personal, satisfyingly communal.

We need the shared celebration of art:
creativity that resides in all of us and feels
like a prayer to happiness.

We are troubadours who need each other's
music—to soar on currents of another's
inspiration, catch beauty that floats
through air, enters the body, spirals down
into the depths of who we are.

I once witnessed newborn twins, moments old,
resting on their mother's chest.
One twin touches the hand of the other,
and that twin grasps the hand that is offered—
holds on.

MIA MING

A newborn left at hospital's door.
The only offense, born a girl.
One of three hundred in a Chinese
orphanage—rows and rows of cribs.

Now she dances on the shores
of Marrowstone Island, opening her arms
to summer sun, splashing in the waters
of Puget Sound, wrapping herself around
mother's legs like seaweed.

I wonder if Asian images, quiet as tidal pools,
ripple with remembered words,
words collected like broken shells
during those first ten months of life,
as a freshet of newfound language
cascades from her lips.

THE LOST CHILDREN

They are hidden in plain sight and they are lonely.
They wander in a forest of neglect searching

for crumbs that lead back to mother, to father.
They nibble left-overs, scraps of attention,

that don't nourish or fill the void of their needs.
They know they are alone. They know no one

is listening. They know they are second best.
Where will they find comfort?

They are like flowers that wilt before they can bloom,
stars with no one to admire their twinkle.

These little ones orbit around parents who can't
seem to kick an endless addiction to phones.

I am heart-broken for the beautiful forsaken children.
They hold onto their secrets, hostages in a silent world

of distracted captors.

TOO SOON

. . . life has to be lived before we can know what it is.
~ Lisel Mueller

What of the infants—those who leave us too soon?
They only taste the air, tiny sips from fragile teacups.

What can they know of life? Touch of skin to skin.
Swaddled in warmth. A song in rhythm

to a loved one's breath. Soft light. The scent
of a familiar body that promises safety.

Enough for those of us who linger?

THE PLAYING FIELD

He is nine years old—nine innings
and the playing field before him.
His mitt a new Spalding 42-263,
stiff and awkward, yet to be formed.
Anointed with shoe oil, then repetitious
chuck of the baseball into the pocket
until a cup forms and the mitt,
which must fit loosely, conforms
to the hand; an extension of the hand
to snag the high ones, get down low
and scoop grounders.

And isn't this what we all want?
To lose our awkwardness, to be anointed
with that which softens us, makes us
more pliable; conforming to fit
who we are meant to be, yet fitting
loosely, extending to the high ones,
to the grounders, the inscrutable
playing field before us?

OPTICAL ILLUSION

The eye receives color, shape,
and light, but the eye does not
recognize certain shades of gray—
the dimming of certainties,
pale fluttering questions,
shifting kaleidoscopic choices.

The eye cannot identify
the hard shape of loss,
the void of loneliness,
or a tight circle of friends.

The eye admits light, but holds it
for its own purposes. It cannot
perceive how sunlight pierces
the prisms of raindrops causing
colors to explode, or that I see sunlight
flicker through eucalyptus leaves
when my lids are closed. It cannot
know what the heart squeezes
out of every beat—the red blood
of wonder.

THE QUESTION OF HAPPINESS

Does happiness carry danger
in its heart?

A dagger waiting to plunge into
the chest of joy.

An affliction we suffer in the midst
of unbroken contentment.

Perhaps we turn from those quiet moments
that need no explanation, elevated moments

that rush toward bliss, as if too much
happiness portends misfortune.

Love rises to the edge of risk,
balances on the possibility of loss—

a journey down an uncertain road,
no promises along the way.

Don't we owe it to ourselves and others
to pursue happiness?

Walking into the sun, I can't see
what's ahead, can't see into the shadows

until I'm in them.

WAITING FOR WHAT'S TO COME

The sky broods over the inlet, deepens
to the exact color of an Italian plum,
then thunder cracks the silence
the way ripeness splits the plum.

Why do we hold our breath as we wait
for what's to happen? Do we think
we can stop the turning of the world,
the rotation of events about to occur?

We wait, bound in a cocoon of unknown
expectation—a flash of excitement,
a flare of danger.

Lightning blinks its electrifying beauty
and the first drops fall, a gentle patter,
a rendition of grace upon a thirsty earth.

Somehow, through all our anxieties
and fears, most outcomes settle somewhere
between the worst and the best.

NIGHT FLIGHT INTO METAPHOR

It's what you would expect to find
in complex, compressed air—poems

hide in plain sight and they
are everywhere.

See the young mother and restless babe,
the umbilical cord barely dry,

their entwined stories yet to be gathered
into a collection.

See how darkness obliterates earth,
and how the moon continues its old tale.

Sip champagne and watch bubbles
escape into the sky. You only think

they are stars. And it's strange, really,
how a rainbow, free from earthbound view,

becomes a full circle, plane
and passengers at the center.

Where else can you experience lightning
zagging nearby, dancing on silver wings?

And the perfect silence, following
the announcement, *Flaps fail to deploy,*

will be landing at an accelerated speed.

The collective sigh of a safe landing.

ESTATE SALE

The newspaper notice could portend
the elegance of English gardens,
gold-rimmed china, crystal goblets
sparkling in candlelight, conversations
prancing around a generous table,
but here in this modest home,
after the children have taken
what they want, strangers consider
an accumulation of what remains.

Kitchen cabinets stand open exposing
half-used boxes of cereal and sugar,
bathroom counters cluttered
with an array of sprays and soaps.

Footprints soil the light carpet,
and on the walls pictures hang askew.
Sunlight streams through a dining room
window, yet the air feels heavy with loss.

A bed stripped of linens, and in the closet
an intimate odor, as if some wisp of a life
remains, floating among limp shirts
with lifeless sleeves, shoes for all occasions
the owner will not attend, a shabby bathrobe
with dangling ties, a walker tucked into a corner.

The shadow of sadness falls across
tools, dishes, bedding, stacks of books,
trinkets from travels, and we know little
of the traveler or the journey, only
what we can imagine from what remains.

AN INSTANT WHEN EVERYTHING CHANGES

Flying kites at Fort Casey and feeling like
a kid, the kite a multi-colored butterfly
with long pink streamers. I hold the tension
as it climbs skyward against the wind
and the sky, oh, the sky—it won't surprise you
to know the sky is that perfect summer blue,
the blue New Yorkers described on nine-eleven.

For an instant a winged shadow passes over,
turns everything dark, and I'm lost in remembering
a coldness that changed who I am.

I hold on to the string, not allowing the beauty
of this day to float away, and think of the Seals
who risked everything to bring twelve boys
out of a flooded cave in Thailand. Their goodness
fills the hollowed-out spaces of my sadness,
a golden beam of saving light.

CORONA

When the invisible becomes real,
we pay attention. How did it happen
we ask, and so suddenly?

In the night sky we praise what we can see: a circle
of light, a visible glow, an enchantment of rarified gases
that take us beyond ourselves into a universe

that challenges and inspires our understanding. Now,
a deadly corona close by, a devious combatant,
exposed and brought to light under a microscope's
glare.

What are we to learn from the chaos of uncertainty?
How can the isolation that defines us bring us together?
When the world is brought to its knees by a hidden

foe, kindness becomes real, bonding a strength.
Like sunlight and wind, our compassion is evident
by the force of its action.

SHELTERING IN PLACE

April, 2020

I want to remember this time,
this time of waiting. We are like
spring bulbs emerging little by little
through the dark earth, holding
future promise tightly within ourselves.

I want to remember the gradual dawning
of danger, how it feels to be removed
from what we knew to be true.

They say suffering involves loss of control.
It is thrust upon us and although I've
settled into this different way of being,
the ache is bone-deep for those taken
beyond a quiet island of isolation.

I want to remember our pressing need
for each other. This yearning to touch,
skin to skin, to authenticate what is
fine and just and joyful.

Now the apple tree is setting blossoms.
A dove is cooing from across the field.
As I rise from my labors in the garden
the calming scent of lavender clings
to my clothes.

THE OLD MARINE

Our neighbor signals
with an American flag
he hangs from his porch
to let us know he is up
and ready to start a new day.

We see it across the field,
a flag he fought to defend,
this old marine, whose wife
died last year. Now he lives
with memories.

This morning I watch him
climb the porch steps,
unsteady, but determined.
I think about his pain

from injuries and multiple
infirmities, but can't begin
to imagine what he endured
all those years ago in Korea,
ascending frozen hills in a brutal
landscape, surrounded and trapped
in the Chosin Reservoir.

QUIET HERO

He is eighty-eight. He is in hospice care.
He has made friends with the oxygen tank
which follows him around, his constant companion.

He loves jazz. He loves a particular jazz pianist.
His family asked him if there was anything
he wanted to do, knowing his time was limited.
He said, *I would like to hear that trio once again.*

They bundle him up, take him to the club
where the trio is playing. Jack Daniels, his drink
of choice—tonight it's ice water spiked with jazz.

Have you ever noticed how some of the elderly
seem to live enclosed in an aura of peace?
It is as if they have had all their questions
answered and are satisfied with the replies.

He is invited to sit in, moved to a chair on stage,
and given a mic. The sweet, steady flow of oxygen
glazes his notes as he croons his favorite song:
On the Sunny Side of the Street.

SPRING SOLSTICE

March 20, 2019

Middle of the night and sleep
a distant horizon. The brightness

of the super moon electrifies
the darkness, an ethereal glow

that defies the hour, and my mind
travels long-forgotten roads,

mostly rural, some bumpy and pot-holed,
to a small town where we grew up

wide-eyed and trusting. We have stayed
in touch, my high school classmates,

dear friends who gather each year by the river
for a reunion. We are old now.

One man, just diagnosed with lung cancer,
says, *It makes me feel better just to see all of you*

and it may be that we see each other as we were:
bobby socks, poodle skirts, hot rods, ducktail hair.

I marvel at how perception defies the years.

HANS CHRISTIAN ANDERSEN

What was he thinking?
The witch's head removed
in a single swipe. The king
and queen ravaged by dogs.

Mean dispensable grandmothers
killed for money; horses whacked
on their heads, the hides sold
for bushels of coins.

Born on the pistil of a flower,
a girl child about to be married off
to an ugly toad.

A lonely duck pecked and harassed
for being different.

In trees monkeys bare their teeth;
the dark forests fill with ominous
shadows, screeching raptors,
and baying hounds.

Because of an abusive father, a barefoot girl
cannot go home, found out in the cold,
frozen to death.

And disguised as an old man, Death carries
children off to a place mothers can't find.

Afraid to get too close, we hold ugliness
and danger at a safe distance, yet we
continue to turn the pages, losing our heads
to the joy of scariness.

DRAGONFLY

As a group they're called a dazzle.
They open windows of imagination,

and the flashing iridescence of sunlight
on fragile wings, the delicate symmetry,

lifts us toward this metaphor in flight.
Blinded by the glare of beauty, a ballet

of grace and elegance, we fail to see
the strong mandible, the sharp edges

of strength that can crush prey
in one bite.

PLACE OF SMOKE AND TIDES

I come to the shore, a reflective place
of self-comfort. I feel the ease of silence,
the soothing chill of a winter day,
the friendly tang of fires
from the campground.

There is something about this place
that allows me to take apart
my grievances, as if a twinkle
of insight rides on the susurrus
of waves faithful to the shore.

This afternoon disappointment curls
around me, and like trying to build
a fire with wet firewood, smolders
and smokes but does not ignite,
unlike anger's hot flame.

Hard to say which causes
the deepest burn.

SETTING THINGS RIGHT

It feels good to set things right
and when we can't, to do
what we can in another way.

The rhythm of knitting needles
lining up stitches in perfect order.
Numbers in the ledger agreeing
at the end of the month.
The smooth vibrations of the old
Massey Ferguson after adjustments
have been made.

This morning, weeding in my herb garden,
I inhale rosemary and conjure images
of the bubbling sauce. Close by, tarragon
for creamy mushroom pasta,
lavender, lovage, and thyme.

A hummingbird comes jazzing by,
its flight an improvisation of zip and dazzle.
This little rufous knows where he's been
and where he's going.

It feels good to set things right
and for a time, right here and now,
I can make things better. The world
feels less tilted and sunlight illuminates
the edges of everything.

WAITING EVERYWHERE

They are moving, this young couple, because
they *haven't been able to make friends*
on the island.

It seems as if friends are waiting everywhere:
cheerful clerks behind counters at the pharmacy
and market, the librarian among the stacks

of books, the postmaster offering a stamp
of approval, a neighbor raising a cup of tea,
the ferry attendant guiding our travels,

and in the fields the company of deer,
herons that congregate during a storm,
the harmonious conversation of bees.

Friendship is like looking at layers of clouds
lit by silvery light, unique arrangements,
there to make of it what we can.

These connections, wrapped in vulnerability,
are not without risk, and loss is a part
of love, yet it may be as simple as this:

a friend is someone who makes you smile.

CIRCLE OF TWO

We need to belong, the way crows ink
their signatures on a tablet of sky

and autumn leaves titter in the wind,
a ballet of take and release.

This pairing, a natural ripening
like the fullness of wheat in midday sun.

Even the extroverted moon, so far distant,
calls and we answer with longing

that seals our lips with thwarted
words. Now rosehips and snowberries

riot in roadside thickets,
a complement of winter contrast,

and in the mountains, bighorn sheep
follow ancient paths to arrive

where they belong.

NOSTALGIA

I wonder why I try so hard to remember
the name of the department store
on the corner, across from the bank,
in the little town where I grew up.

Eunice, a tiny spinster, prim in every way,
presided over perfectly stacked boxes of nylons
and silky slips, blouses, cardigan sweaters.

The store was bare by modern standards,
hardwood floors swept clean, and although
Eunice had a ready smile, her tidiness
was intimidating.

I can picture her so clearly: pretty teeth,
hair parted in the middle and pulled back
into a neat bun. Peter-pan-collared blouse,
pearls, straight skirt, cardigan sweater,
nylons, and brown lace-up shoes.

Perhaps I need the refreshment
of simpler times. How a smile can endure
through the years and the people who nurtured
me in that town rush back to greet me.

THREE

As a bird perched on a frail branch that she feels bending beneath her, still she sings away all the same, knowing she has wings.

~ *Victor Hugo*

THE WITCH OF WHIDBEY ISLAND

She didn't want to cast a spell
of pure evil, more a diluted
distillation—a bubbling mix
of rust and snot and dung,
to remind the islanders
this may not be paradise.

Start with lavender fields,
a bit of blight to temper
the exuberant hue and scent.

Or a few more thorns among
the Nootka roses growing
in hedgerows and thickets
along the country roads.
Surely that will prick
the resilient skin
of their devotion.

Perhaps more fog to obscure
the Olympics viewed from the bluff
above the inlet; yet islanders
seem infatuated with the melancholy
moan of foghorns.

And oh, the prairie, how they
prize the prairie, as if the ploughed
furrows, glistening like shaved
chocolate, and the wheat
and oats and squash and beets
that rise from the fields
satisfy every hunger.

The witch contemplated the shore,
the tide an endless rhythm
sighing and murmuring
contentment. Possibly more
salt, a corrosive, to tarnish
the islander's spirits, but
she watched the beachcombers
spread their arms, taking great
draughts of the salty air as if
they couldn't get enough.
She stirred her brew, stewed
about the disappointing effects.
She hadn't expected to find
impenetrable magical charms
scattered everywhere on the island.

DESIRE

He swam across the cold waters of Deception Pass
to arrive on our island, this four-hundred-pound
young black bear.

This is not Alaska. We are accustomed to sea lions,
seals, and whales in our waters, not bears.
He traveled through our neighborhood,
ate three pounds of bird seed
from a neighbor's yard, and took a nap nearby.

Followed by Department of Fish and Wildlife,
he swam to ten other islands, then returned
to the mainland where they found him
in a tree.

Desire, a wild thing with large paws,
may propel us into unknown waters;
makes us realize how little we know
about ourselves—what we might risk
to satisfy tenacious hungers.

THINGS I KNOW I DON'T LIKE EVEN THOUGH I'VE NEVER TRIED THEM

I like to sit by the sea and write, but would deny myself
the pleasure of standing in the waves to cast a line.

I love to walk, meditate in the green haze of nature,
but without a golf club in my hand.

Bicycling is one of my favorite things,
but not while linked to a motor.

I savor the beauty of mountains, yet have no desire
to dangle from a lift then descend at break-neck speed.

I contemplate the changing moods of clouds, but can't
    imagine
flinging myself through them attached to a billowing chute.

I enjoy music, even dancing, yet would wither
under a disco ball, flashing lights, and noise.

With increasing age, I try to look my best, but shy away
from tattooed eyebrows, fluttering false eyelashes.

Then the obvious: swimming with sharks, smoking a cigar,
eating pickled herring, fish net stockings, short shorts.

Now I fear I have revealed too much of myself.
I won't divulge the things I like to do even though

I know I shouldn't.

PARABLE OF A CARB LOVER

Lola is irresistible in spite of her issues,
which are many.

The eyes of this yellow lab plead,
Love me, just love me.

She arrived at my niece Lauren's house unannounced,
a note tucked into her collar which read, Lola.

The mischief began straightaway when she ate lipstick
from Lauren's purse, then consumed half

of a Papa Murphy's pizza. Her noshing misdeeds
have included an entire loaf of artisan jalapeno bread,

a beautifully decorated loaf of gingerbread,
six double chocolate fudge protein bars,

a blackberry pie left cooling on the counter,
the plate licked clean, having never left the countertop.

A loaf of bread stolen from a neighbor's garage,
cuticle oils, hand lotion, anything that smells slightly
sweet,

candy left out during the holidays, anything edible
under or on the Christmas tree.

Lauren believes Lola is *a gift from God. She is so imperfect*
she teaches me over and over, no matter how imperfect

and flawed I am, I am loved.

DEEP THINKER

My friend says, *You must have a deep interior life*
and I say, Indeed I do.

I wonder, as I pass the dairy case, how it is possible
to have a product labeled *nonfat half and half.*

I ponder why health food stores look more like
pharmacies: boxes of tablets, bottles of pills.

I think about the intricacies of human bodies
as I sneeze while driving down the freeway

at seventy miles an hour. Not a good time
to close my eyes.

This involuntary response, apparently,
keeps eyeballs from disengaging.

I've thought about that a lot, and why
on PCs you have to go to Start to Shut Down.

I wonder if Emily Dickinson ever used words
like *stench or bum or burp.*

And I wonder why, when I'm feeling discouraged,
playing with words peps me up.

MIDDLE OF THE NIGHT MUSINGS

You don't need a reason to be happy.
I don't know who said that—oh,
I think it was me.

I'm not obliged to notice how
cherry cream scones on the tea tray
wave Scottish flags.

How my sweetie and I share a compass,
directed toward an unmistakable magnet,
its needle steady and true.

How the newborn curls on my chest
in sleep, swaddled in a blanket
of trust.

How snow comes in the night,
hushes the island, cozies us
around the hearth's crackling flames.

How a hummingbird appears, a flash
of jazz in the midst of winter's
soliloquy.

How the deer come every morning
to my window, plead with luminous
eyes for me to bring them apples.

Or how raindrops bead on the window,
gather and run together, a cascade
of opalescent harmony.

How sunrise burns its greeting into the day
and sunset's disappearing radiance
signals rest.

I believe you don't need a reason
to be happy, but having reasons
is a delicious start.

POET'S WISH LIST

Arrange stained-glass words that scatter
light, like the blessing of rainbows
and the lessons of rain.

Cobble together a contented tune,
a notion to dance in the midst
of uncompromising gloom.

Excavate an innermost site,
sift through rubble to unearth
a thought that glitters.

Burn negatives, old hurts
that keep on hurting, stored
in memory's broken box.

Settle in reverie's pocket,
comfortable among the silver coins
jingling there.

Start a fire with kindling and flint,
a breath to make it flame
and glow.

FABRIC WORLD

I meander through the aisles of the quiet,
almost deserted, shop. Luxuriate
in the finger-slide of satin, taffeta, and tulle;

choose a bolt of dimity, place
it on the counter to be measured and cut.
The clerk, clipboard and pencil in hand, says,

I'll be with you in a minute. I wait,
praise my patience, while she completes
her task, then tidies up the counter.

She comes over, stands in front of me.
Did you take a number? I look around.
No one else in sight. A number?

She points to a metal container
at the end of the counter, a red paper
tongue hanging from its mouth.

I walk six steps, tear off the numbered tag,
walk back, hand it to her. She turns,
picks up a microphone and coming

from the store's loudspeaker I hear,
Calling number thirty-nine.

I raise my hand, beckon her over,
That would be me.

RED

It muscles its way into your body
coursing through vessels pulsing
with energy, lighting up your brain,
fueling trillions of subservient cells.

It shoots a flaming arrow into the heart
of passion, accelerates heartbeats
and a multitude of hungers, saturates
the rose.

It dominates the bullseye with boldness,
a *bring it on* attitude ready to do business.

Red will smack you in the face, a temper
rising. Throw water on it; it dilutes
to sweetness, a little girl's pink umbrella
opening out.

The gentler side goes deeper
into darkness, the richness and quiet
intensity of a burgundy wine.

And there in a lather of clouds, a flash
of brilliance as a red-tailed hawk
angles toward the sun.

STAMP OF APPROVAL

It would be so much easier if we came stamped
with who we are meant to be.

If, at the time the umbilical cord is severed,
an indelible word would appear, tattooed in blood,
ever to remain:

farmer, engineer, artist, oceanographer, homemaker,
mathematician, violin maker, novelist, race car driver,
theologian, astronomer . . .

Thing about it—during your midlife crisis,
when you sit staring at your navel, thinking
you are the great philosopher and will figure it out,
you have only to look a little closer to discover
who you are meant to be.

THE CLARINET AND THE CLARINETIST

I treated you with respect,
even though you were old
and used when you first
came into my life. I was young
and hadn't had much experience.

I wasn't a great player, but I found
you had good tone and I had
agile fingering. By the time
we were in the high school band
we were awarded first chair.

All those years—practice sessions,
concerts, solos, a woodwind quartet,
and even the zaniness of a German
oompah band.

Now that I'm older I realize
I never really liked you, especially
the texture of the reed in my mouth,
the smell of olive oil on your corks,
your squawks at inopportune times,
and the disgusting business of swabbing
spit from your innards: a musical
colonoscopy.

So, it's time for me to move on.
I know you will find someone
who will appreciate your qualities
and give you the respect you deserve.
I want to be perfectly honest with you—
I'm attracted to the silvery lilt of the flute.

VARIATIONS ON A RAVEN

I am being harassed by a bird—
a small brown tedious nondescript bird.

I have a slight bird phobia
and without getting into my rather boring

psychological history just let me say
I put a wooden salad bowl over my head

when I venture outside and the great horned owl
is perched on our roof.

How a tiny bird, not much bigger than a pill bottle,
could drive me to potential need of medication

is something to ponder. It comes every day.
It comes several times a day. It waits

in the honeysuckle for me to come home
so it can resume its dastardly deeds.

The bird is enamored of mirrors, but it also
admires itself over the entire surface

of my shiny black car, leaving a trail of muddy
footprints and fecal droppings in its conscientious

pursuit of self. Like a vain starlet, the bird is in love
with its image and the attraction of bling and glitter.

Rubber snakes, garbage bags, bright fluttery
streamers, and noisy human outbursts

have done nothing to thwart the persistent bird.
I contemplate the life span of this avian monster

and perhaps *Tis the wind and nothing more,*
but I hear something whispering, *Evermore.*

THE CONVENTION

We know a storm is imminent when the seagulls hold their convention. Hundreds gather, tightly packed, in the middle of an inland field, talking all at once. Have they not heard of courtesy? Protocol? Robert's Rules of Order? One, all fluff and dander with a rude open mouth and flapping wings, is intent on out-shouting the others. Some are haughty, strutting around on scrawny legs, looking down their long bills at the other gulls that seem like reasonable creatures, but are obviously, in some obtuse way, inferior. As a group, they appear to support individual rights until one gull acquires a fractured clam and then there is a clamorous attempt to redistribute the wealth. They are not able to deflect the storm or turn the tide. They give the impression they find comfort and a sense of safety in being grouped together, talking the same language, even if they don't accomplish anything. I wonder if they are Democrats or Republicans. They certainly are not associated with The Green Party. These delegates pollute.

CAULIFLOWER SOUP FOR BREAKFAST

I have an extravagant fondness for vegetables.
Some view this as slightly abnormal.

Last night, for dinner, I ate Romano beans,
sugar snap peas, golden beets, carrots,

radishes, and sweet green peppers,
fresh from my garden.

I swoon over cauliflower, broccoli,
red and green cabbage, and Brussels sprouts.

In the spring, without question—asparagus
with every meal—in omelets, pastas,

with deviled eggs. Vine-ripened tomatoes:
beefsteak, Roma, and sun golds.

Corn on the cob, kale, Swiss chard,
and lettuce of every description.

During winter months I turn to turnips,
rutabagas, and parsnips without bias.

I never tire of potatoes, the old ugly stepsisters
of the garden, transformed into hash browns,

or bakers with fancy toppings; fingerlings creamed
with peas, others scalloped with ham, steamed

with butter and parsley. I've been known to save
vegetables left-over from dinner to enjoy

the next morning for breakfast, and I will admit
that once, in an upscale restaurant,

I bargained with my sister:
Her creamed spinach for my *crème brulee.*

BABY TOES

My mind turns cartwheels
when I think of those little feet,
hot and sweaty, the toes lined up
like cannoli arranged on a dessert tray.

Only a memory now, my sons' feet, not exactly
barges, more like paddle boats off to new
adventures. Those young men would be
embarrassed, yes, mortified, if they knew
of my sentimental musings.

But a mother's memory is what it needs to be
to hold the beloveds close. I remember
their belly-laughs, how their tummies
jiggled with laughter when I kissed those toes.

GENDER BIAS

No girls allowed, but
we didn't care—those
grimy boys, grubbing
in the dust of the playground.

Recess bell and they scrambled
to the same spot, scribing
a circle in the dirt and tossing
in their marbles.

We heard the names: Aggies,
Cat's Eyes, Bennington's,
Bonker, Popper, Bumboozer,
Biggie. The Steelie, a shiny
ball bearing, a gift of grace
from a father's repair project,
seemed high and mighty
among the fragile glass spheres.

The boys crowded around the circle,
pulling shooters out of their pockets
and each had a favorite flicking technique:
first finger, middle finger, or thumb.
A strong shot was needed to knock
a marble out of the ring.

We girls, who danced and sang inside
the rhymical ropes of Double Dutch,
were definitely outside the ring
and glad of it.

EBEY'S PRAIRIE

We live on a prairie in the middle of an island.
Our prairie, a small tray of land bordered
by a cemetery that cradles the pioneers,
ends at a bluff that drops to the sea.

Where indigenous people once harvested camas,
native grasses are all but gone, tamed into fields
of wheat and barley and oats.

Island wind blows over the prairie.
The crops and grasses that remain
rise to its will in green and gold waves
that rush to meet those rolling in from the sea.

Rich prairie soil yields to the plow, allows
for growth. Like the seeds that sprout
there, we have a chance to ripen and grow,
open to a larger force that shapes us,
moving us to something beyond ourselves.

THE GARDENER POET

> *How could you be an artist if you didn't explore your own inner life?*
>
> *~ Stanley Kunitz*

He *lived in the layers, not on the litter,*
and he went deep into a lake of awareness,
fed by clear underground springs.

It is not enough to be dazzled
by beauty, but to gain sight
into what it means.

Everything has meaning. *The universe*
is a continuous web. Touch it at any point
and the whole web quivers.

He explored the caves of what we know,
followed the curve of what we cannot know,
dim shadows flickering around a fire of insight.

He spoke the language of the wordless,
each poem a revelation leading back
to the source of who he was.

He said he was just *passing through,*
but he planted a garden of elegant words
giving his language unending life.

THE ELEGANCE OF AGEING

Old Barn, Watercolor
~ Keith Fakkema

The old barn stands alone, its weathered boards
a testament to the hot breath of summers past,
the pounding fists of winter storms.

Early morning, I hear a rooster crow and milk pails
clanking, see the dance of dust motes in the loft,
remember the pungent smell of fresh manure,
grain in burlap sacks, the warmth of cows
fitting their heads through stanchions
at milking time.

Now the barn, once sheltering,
is open to sky. What do the empty
spaces say? Silence lingers like rests
between notes of a cherished song.

Some would claim this relic from another
time has slipped beyond its usefulness, yet
it stands open to air and light. Swallows
fly in and out and find a home.

THE OVER SIXTY SOFTBALL LEAGUE

All shapes and sizes, they scatter
onto the field. Here where summer
pushes the mercury into the eighties
they wear shorts and purple jerseys,
knee braces, and mismatched
lucky socks.

These boys of summers past
have what it takes to get the job done:
home runs, double plays, popping
the Texas Leaguer.

Their days as young sprouts
when all was growth and adventure
are traced in their movements:
the rhythm of the pitcher's grace,
the extra spurt toward home base,
the way the body eases
under a fly ball.

They win the game at the top
of the sixth, result of the mercy
rule (fourteen to two). Winners
of more than the tournament title,
these guys are champs.
They draw together
the way swallows gather before
they leave, check the nesting place
and are gone.

Wives from the opposing side
sit in the shade and knit.
After the game one of them says,
Thank God we lost. Now we can
go home.

WHY HAVE FAVORITES?

A house on a hill. A leather-bound book.

Lilies of the Valley. Swans.

New-mown hay. Cezanne's art.

The porch on a summer day. White peaches.

The Secret Garden. A child's laughter.

Walking in fog. Lavender.

Amadeus, the movie. Fresh Dungeness crab.

Louie singing *It's a Wonderful World*.

Snowflakes. Rum raisin ice cream.

That blue-green color deep in the swirls
of Deception Pass.

Sunlight through stained glass windows.

Oscar Peterson's *Hymn of Freedom*.

If you don't have favorites, how do you
make each day special?

JUST BECAUSE

He is waiting for the ferry with his grandma,
a cute four-year-old, shoehorn in hand.

Grandpa gave him the shoehorn and now
the world glitters with possibilities.
Do you use that shoehorn? I ask
and he slides down off the bench
to demonstrate. Shoe off,
shoehorn applied, shoe on.

He has it with him wherever he goes,
his grandma says. Of all the treasures
a child could choose, a shoehorn?

It's goofy in a sweet way and I wonder
what it portends.

Fashion designer?

Politician? To be prepared if he must
slip in and out of a situation quickly.

Big shoes to fill?

I love this kid! This is a one-of-a-kind guy
who knows his own mind,
yet I consider reasons for this little boy's
obsession with a shoehorn and maybe
there isn't one and maybe that's the point—
there doesn't need to be a reason
for who and what we love.

THIS TIME TOGETHER

When I asked him about his journey
he said, *I feel as if I'm about ready*
to take the first step.

What does that mean? Anticipation
of something better? Movement
in a new direction? Excitement
from a fresh insight?

You travel by words, he says,
I travel by landmarks.

It's true in so many ways. I read
road signs, arrange symbols on a page
from the inside out.

He studies geological formations
and architecture; builds structures
from the bottom up.

I don't need to understand to know
it works. We fill in the spaces
of each other.

JOURNEY HOME

How an island birthed from upheaval,
crimped at the center as if permanently
lashed by pain, battered by tireless winds
and monumental waves can offer solace

is the question. Yet the island welcomed
me when I returned after a long time away.
I'm lulled to sleep in the mash of wind and sea,
a lullaby that sounds achingly familiar.

I find my grandmother's name in an attendance
book from the one-room 1880's schoolhouse
on the hill. I visit the old church where my great-uncle
bent with hammer and saw, tipped up walls.

I walk the trail that follows the bluff, light
rising and falling, darkness descending,
twisted storm-driven evergreens claiming
purchase high above the sea.

The moody clouds and fogs, a stillness
that is silent praise. I am here to listen,
yet silence holds its secrets in a deep pouch
just beyond my reach.

Perhaps it is more than a journey home,
this need to know how we fit, where we belong.
I am caught in the paradox of wanting to know,
but enticed by the mystery of not knowing.

THE LONESOME TIME

Sunday afternoons, when we were kids,
our father took us for rides on country backroads.
We twisted around mountains, followed
the curve and chuckle of rivers, passed through
cool shadows in deep canyons, and skirted the coast.

Whenever we drove across Deception Pass Bridge
onto Whidbey Island, at a certain place, in an open field,
on a bluff overlooking Admiralty Inlet, my father
would say, *I'd like to build a house right here someday.*

He died when he was fifty-seven, too soon
for that dream to settle into reality. Now,
years later, I live just down the road
from that open field, on a bluff, overlooking
Admiralty Inlet. His grandchildren
and great-grandchildren come to visit.
They love the island as he did, as I do . . .

I scan the inlet for incoming vessels
as evening light delegates passage
to memories. It is the lonesome time,
just before darkness sets in.

THE SCENT OF MEMORIES

The freshness of summer drifts through
my bedroom window and, for a moment,
I'm suspended in time, as if I'd forgotten
the scent of grass, the fragrant
exhalations of earth.

I remember my young self
almost hidden in tall grass, fingering
bleeding hearts that grew wild
and somehow touched the wild
yearnings of my naive heart.

Lying in the backyard on the cushiony lawn,
a dreamy canopy of clouds overhead,
I transformed them into whatever
I wanted them, and me, to be.

How is it we let go of the simple things
that ground us—forget the smell of dark soil,
of mosses, leaves, and clover?

I wander with the child, the young girl,
the woman, a wife, a mother; my life
a vine, twining around seasons
of loss and joy.

Now the sweet silence of twilight,
the purple glow of approaching darkness
a gentle comfort.

ACKNOWLEDGMENTS

Grateful acknowledgment is made to the editors of the following publications in which these poems first appeared.

"Apples of Winter," *Quill and Parchment,* 2020

"Art Nouveau," *What's to be Done with Beauty,* Creative Justice Press, 2012

"Baby Toes," *Your Daily Poem,* 2020

"Corona," *American Writers Review,* 2020

"Ebey's Landing," *Mizmor Anthology,* Poetica Publishing, 2020

"Eventide," *Your Daily Poem,* 2020

"Fabric World," *Show Us Your Papers Anthology, Main Street Rag,* 2020

"Ominous Beauty," *Mountain Anthology*, Middle Creek Publishing, 2020

"The Clarinet and Clarinetist," Third Place Prize, *Artists Embassy International Dancing Poetry Festival*, 2020

"The Convention," *Clackamas Review,* 2004

"The Lesson of Plums," *Adanna: Women and War, a Tribute to Adrienne Rich, 2013; Night Beyond Black,* MoonPath Press, 2016

"Winter Art," *Quill and Parchment,* 2020

My deepest gratitude to Diane Stone, Sheryl Clough, and Teresa Wiley for continued support and friendship as we share our mutual love of poetry.

My heartfelt thanks to Lana Ayers, editor, for her kind and perceptive recommendations and to Tonya Namura for her beautiful design work.

As always, thanks to my dear friends and family who are the source of inspiration for many of my poems, and generously share their gifts of love, light, and laughter.

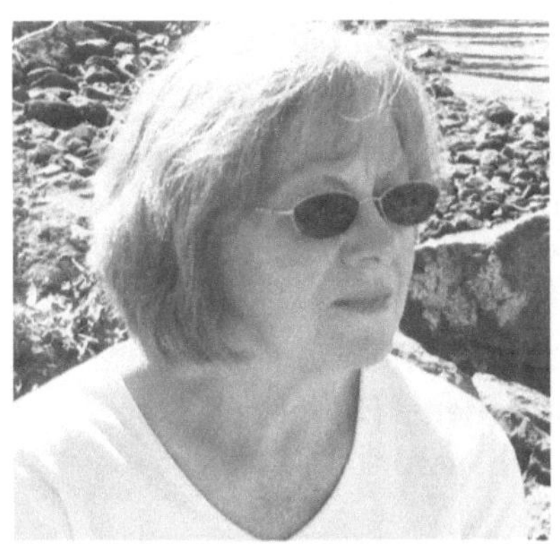

ABOUT THE AUTHOR

Lois Parker Edstrom, a retired nurse, is the author of two chapbooks and four full length collections of poetry. *What Brings Us To Water* won the 2010 Poetica Publishing Chapbook Award. *What's To Be Done With Beauty* received the Creative Justice Award in 2012. Full length books include *Night Beyond Black*, MoonPath Press, 2016; *Glint*, MoonPath Press, 2019; *Road Signs and Hobo Marks*, Cyberwit, India, 2020, and *The Lesson of Plums*, MoonPath Press, 2020.

She has received two Hackney National Literary Awards, the Outrider Press Grand Prize, and the Westmoreland Award. Her poems have appeared in various anthologies and in literary journals such as *Clackamas Literary Review, Floating Bridge Review, Rock & Sling, Mobius, American Writers Review,* and *Adanna.* In 2017 and 2019, Edstrom's work received nominations for a Pushcart Prize and the Washington State Book Award.

Three of her poems have been read by Garrison Keillor on *The Writer's Almanac*, and a poem was featured in *American Life in Poetry*. In 2016 Edstrom's career in nursing and her poetic passion coalesced when her poem, *Choices We Make When We Are Too Young to Make Them*, appeared in *Poems in the Waiting Room*, a publication furnished to hospitals and doctors' offices in New Zealand. Her poetry has been translated into Braille, and has also been adapted to dance by the Bellingham Repertory Dance Company. The natural beauty of Whidbey Island, where she lives with her husband, inspires much of her work.

www.ingramcontent.com/pod-product-compliance
Lightning Source LLC
Chambersburg PA
CBHW021333060726
47591CB00006B/1991